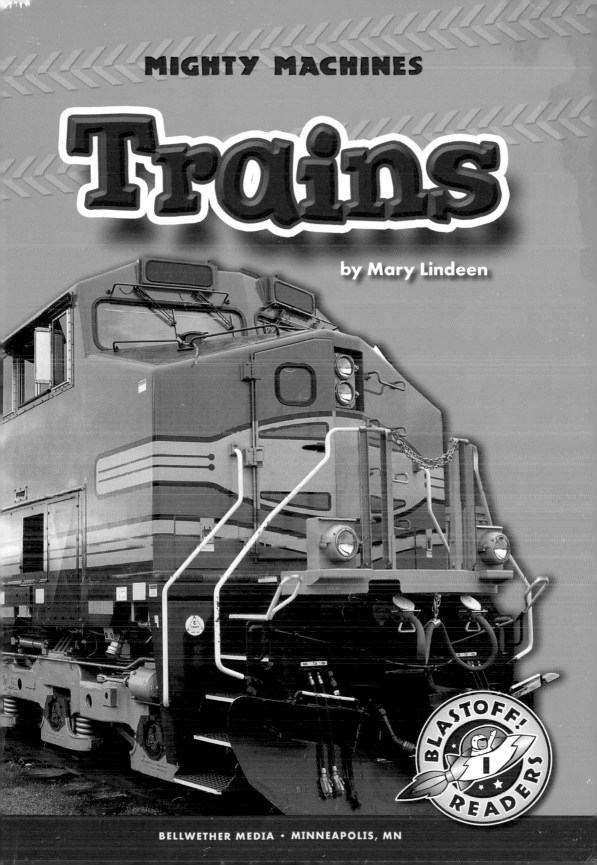

MIGHTY MACHINES

Trains

by Mary Lindeen

BELLWETHER MEDIA • MINNEAPOLIS, MN

BLASTOFF! READERS

Note to Librarians, Teachers, and Parents:

Blastoff! Readers are carefully developed by literacy experts and combine standards-based content with developmentally-appropriate text.

Level 1 provides the most support through repetition of high-frequency words, light text, predictable sentence patterns, and strong visual support.

Level 2 offers early readers a bit more challenge through varied simple sentences, increased text load, and less repetition of high frequency words.

Level 3 advances early-fluent readers toward fluency through increased text and concept load, less reliance on visuals, longer sentences, and more literary language.

Level 4 builds reading stamina by providing more text per page, increased use of punctuation, greater variation in sentence patterns, and increasingly challenging vocabulary.

Level 5 encourages children to move from "learning to read" to "reading to learn" by providing even more text, varied writing styles, and less familiar topics.

Whichever book is right for your reader, Blastoff! Readers are the perfect books to build confidence and encourage a love of reading that will last a lifetime!

This edition first published in 2007 by Bellwether Media, Inc.

No part of this publication may be reproduced in whole or in part without written permission of the publisher. For information regarding permission, write to Bellwether Media, Inc., Attention: Permissions Department, 5357 Penn Avenue South, Minneapolis, MN 55419.

Library of Congress Cataloging-in-Publication Data
Lindeen, Mary.
  Trains / by Mary Lindeen.
    p. cm. — (Blastoff! Readers) (Mighty machines)
Summary: "Simple text and supportive full-color photographs introduce young readers to trains. Intended for kindergarten through third grade"—Provided by publisher.
  Includes bibliographical references and index.
  ISBN 978-1-60014-062-4 (hardcover : alk. paper)
  1. Railroads—Juvenile literature. I. Title.
  TF148.L54 2007
  625.2—dc22   2006035264

Printed in the United States of America, North Mankato, MN.   110110   1178

Contents

A train is a
big machine
that moves
on tracks.

A train has **cars**.
The cars on
a **passenger
train** carry
people.

The cars on
a **freight train**
carry **cargo**.

A train has an **engine**. The engine pulls the cars.

A train has an
engineer.
The engineer
drives the train.

The engine has a **whistle**. The whistle tells people the train is coming.

This **bullet train** goes very fast!

This **subway train** goes under the ground.

A train stops
at a **station**.
All aboard!

Glossary

bullet train—a very fast train

cargo—things that are carried by trains, ships, planes, or trucks

cars—vehicles with wheels

engine—a kind of vehicle that pulls train cars on tracks

engineer—the driver of a train

freight train—a train that carries things from one place to another

passenger train—a train that carries people from one place to another

station—a stopping place

subway train—a train that goes under the ground

whistle—a tube that makes a high, loud sound when you blow air through it

To Learn More

AT THE LIBRARY

Booth, Philip. *Crossing*. Cambridge, Mass.: Candlewick, 2001.

Brown, Margaret Wise. *Two Little Trains*. New York: HarperCollins, 2001.

Kuklin, Susan. *All Aboard!: A True Train Story*. London, UK: Orchard, 2003.

O'Brien, Patrick. *Steam, Smoke, and Steel: Back in Time with Trains*. Watertown, Mass.: Charlesbridge, 2000.

ON THE WEB
Learning more about mighty machines is as easy as 1, 2, 3.

1. Go to www.factsurfer.com

2. Enter "mighty machines" into search box.

3. Click the "Surf" button and you will see a list of related web sites.

With factsurfer.com, finding more information is just a click away.

Index

The photographs in this book are reproduced through the courtesy of: Furchin, front cover; Roy Toft/Getty Images, p. 5; Angelo Cavalli/Getty Images, p. 7; Lester Lefkowitz/Getty Images, p. 9; Louie Schoeman, p. 11; Visions of America, LLC/Alamy, p. 13; Digicanon, p. 15; Orion Press/Getty Images, p. 17; Philip Lange, p. 19; Robert Nickelsberg/Getty Images, p. 21.

DATE DUE

GAYLORD   PRINTED IN U.S.A.